Made by Minty

I Talk You Talk Press

ISBN: 978-4-910971-17-9

www.italkyoutalk.com

info@italkyoutalk.com

CONTENTS

I Talk You Talk Press

CHAPTER ONE

Minty is a fashion design student. She loves to sew. She makes all her own clothes. Her clothes are very unique and stylish. Many people look at her on the street. Sometimes people ask her, "Where did you buy that dress? I want one like it." Minty always answers, "Sorry. I didn't buy it. I made it myself."

But then Minty will have another idea, and she will make herself a new jacket or skirt or dress. She often says, "I have too many clothes."

She shares an apartment with her friend, Dina. The apartment is small. Minty's bedroom is full of clothes. She also keeps clothes in Dina's bedroom.

Dina doesn't worry. She's a junior policewoman. She's not interested in fashion. "I have my uniform to wear to work," she says. "And I have jeans and sweaters for the weekend. I don't need more clothes."

One weekend, Minty goes to visit her parents. She stays with them on Friday and Saturday night. It's dark and raining when Minty returns to the apartment on Sunday night.

Dina is away at a training course, she thinks as she climbs the stairs. *The apartment will be cold. I will have some soup and toast and go to bed.*

When Minty gets to the apartment she is surprised. The door is open.

Did Dina come back? Why are there no lights on? Why didn't she shut the door? Then she sees that the door lock is broken.

Minty walks into the apartment. *Oh no! Someone has been in here!*

Drawers and cupboards are open. There are things all over the floor.

This is terrible! I'm pleased I had my computer with me, thinks Minty. *And Dina took hers as well. I must call the police. But first, I'll call Dina and tell her.*

Minty calls Dina. "I can't come back," says Dina. "You must call the police. Will you be OK?"

"Yes," says Minty. "I'm too scared to stay here tonight. But after the police leave, I'll go and stay with my friend Kirsten."

"What did the robbers take?" asks Dina.

"Nothing," says Minty. "The TV is still here."

Dina says, "Did they take your sewing machine?"

"I don't know. I didn't look!"

Minty hurries to her bedroom. Her sewing machine is there, but all her clothes are gone!

She looks in Dina's bedroom. There are jeans and T shirts and sweaters all over the floor, but Minty's beautiful dresses, skirts, tops, and jackets are gone!

"My sewing machine is here, but all my clothes are gone!" she says to Dina.

"That's terrible," says Dina. "Did they take my clothes?"

"Uh, no," says Minty.

"Well maybe the police should look for robbers who like fashion! I can't come back for a month. Please be careful. Please don't worry."

Minty calls the police. Two policemen come to the apartment. They ask Minty many questions. They take photographs. They are very kind.

Then one policeman says, "We will try to find the people who did this. But there are many robberies like this. You say all your clothes are gone. Were they very expensive designer models?"

"No," says Minty. "I made them myself."

"It's very strange," says the policeman. "Your TV is very old. I can understand why they didn't take it. But why take clothes?"

The policemen fix the broken lock. "You must get a professional to come tomorrow and change it," they say.

They go away.

Minty calls Kirsten. "Can I stay with you tonight?" she asks.

CHAPTER TWO

The next day, Minty goes back to the apartment and cleans everything. She looks at her sewing machine. *Why didn't the robbers take it?* she thinks. *It's a very good machine. But I bought it from a second-hand shop. It's old and heavy. Maybe they didn't want to carry it down the stairs.*

Minty calls the lock company. A man comes and puts a new lock on the door. He gives Minty the keys. "This is a very strong lock," he says. "It will be very difficult for someone to break into your apartment now."

Now that there is a new lock on the door and everything is tidy, I feel OK. I'll stay here, thinks Minty.

Dina is still away on her training course. She will not come back for four weeks.

Minty goes to classes at the college. She sees Kirsten every day. They often have lunch together.

Life is normal, but Minty is a little lonely. She misses Dina, and she misses her clothes!

"I have nothing to wear!" she says to Kirsten.

Kirsten laughs. "That's not bad news! It's good news! You can make new clothes. We don't have classes this afternoon. Let's take the bus and go to Shelton."

Kirsten and Minty go to Shelton. It's a small town next to the sea. It's winter, so there are no tourists. The streets are almost empty. They walk around the town. They look in the shops.

Kirsten goes to the same college as Minty, but she is not interested in fashion. She wants to be an interior designer. She wants to help people make the rooms in their houses beautiful.

Kirsten sees a shop that sells curtains and cushions. It is called Alice's Home Design. "Let's go in there," she says.

They walk into the shop. An older woman is standing on a chair. She is trying to hang some curtains to make a display.

"I'm sorry," she says. "I'm Alice, but I can't help you at the moment. Please look around."

"Can we help you?" asks Kirsten. "That chair looks dangerous. Maybe you will fall."

"Yes, please!" says Alice. "My assistant is a tall young man. He always hangs the displays. But he broke his leg, and now I have no one to help me. There is a ladder in the storeroom, but it is too heavy for me to move."

The girls get the ladder. There are curtains all over the floor. "What do you want us to do?" asks Minty.

Alice is sitting on the chair. "I don't know. I'm so tired today, I can't think. I have no ideas."

Kirsten is a little nervous, but she says, "I think you should put all the modern curtains together on this wall. The curtains with flowers on them can go in the shop window. We can put cushions in the window too."

"Maybe that's a good idea," says Alice. "Please do something. My shop is a mess and I feel bad."

Kirsten is excited. *This is perfect. I know what will look good. This is my chance to use my ideas,* she thinks.

She tells Minty what to do. They make a beautiful display in the window, and another display on the wall.

Alice is very pleased. "You are amazing!" she says. "It's wonderful. You are so clever."

"Not me," laughs Minty. "I was the worker. Kirsten told me what to do."

"I must pay you," says Alice.

"No," says Kirsten. "It was fun. I enjoyed it."

"What about your friend? She worked very hard. Maybe I can give her some money."

They look around. Minty has disappeared. "Where has she gone?" asks Alice.

Kirsten sees Minty. She is at the back of the shop. They walk to the back of the shop to talk to Minty. She is looking at some curtains.

They are very strange. The pattern on the curtains is monkeys and parrots.

"I like these," she says.

"What!" Alice is very surprised. "They are too strange. A very rich man in this town ordered them. He paid me for them. But when he came to get them, he didn't like them. He went away. I don't know what to do with them. No one will want to buy them."

"I love them," says Minty. "But I guess they are very expensive."

Alice laughs. "You can have them for free. I wanted to pay you for your work. But if you want those curtains…."

"Yes please!" says Minty. "I'll make a long coat. It will be wonderful!"

Kirsten looks at her phone. "We must go! The last bus leaves soon."

Kirsten and Minty hurry to the bus. They are carrying the curtains in a big bag. It is heavy, but Kirsten is pleased. *Minty lost all her clothes. It was very sad. But now she will make a new coat. It will make her happy,* she thinks.

Back at the shop, Alice is looking at the curtain displays. *They are very good,* she thinks. *That young woman has very good ideas. I would like her to come and work for me. But I don't even know her name or where she lives!*

CHAPTER THREE

Minty makes the long coat. She likes it very much. But she is sad about her other clothes.

She tells everyone she is OK. But her mother is worried. She calls Minty and says, "You worked so hard to make your beautiful clothes. You are unhappy. I want you to have a treat. I am sending you tickets for the national fashion show."

Minty is very excited. Her mother sends tickets and aeroplane tickets for two people to go to the biggest fashion show of the year.

She calls Dina. "Would you like to come with me?"

Dina laughs. "Thank you! But I'm on my course, and anyway I don't want to go to a fashion show."

Minty asks Kirsten. "Do you want to come to the national fashion show with me? My mother is paying for everything."

"Wow! Yes please!" says Kirsten.

Minty makes some new clothes to wear to the fashion show.

Minty and Kirsten fly to the big city. They stay in a small hotel. They go to the fashion show.

On the last afternoon they are sitting watching the models wearing the clothes by a very famous designer.

"This has been so much fun!' says Minty.

Kirsten doesn't answer. She is looking at a woman sitting in the front row.

Then she says, "Minty! That woman with the long red hair is wearing your jacket!"

Minty looks. "Yes, she is! I don't believe it!"

As soon as the show is over, they hurry outside, and wait next to the door.

When the woman with the long red hair comes out, they walk over to her.

"Excuse me," says Minty. "You are wearing my jacket!"

The woman smiles. "This is my jacket. Did you buy one like it?"

"No," says Kirsten. "There's only one jacket like that. It's unique. My friend made it."

"Oh," says the woman. "You are very clever! I love it. Many people admire it. Do you have other clothes to sell? I'd like to see them."

"No," says Minty. "I only make clothes for myself."

"Where did you get that jacket?" asks Kirsten.

The woman looks surprised. "I bought it online."

"But that jacket was stolen from my apartment!" says Minty.

"Oh," says the woman. She takes the jacket off. "It's yours. Please take it."

This woman is very nice, thinks Minty. *It's not her fault.*

"No," she says to the woman. "Please keep it. I'm pleased you like it. I'll make another one for myself."

"Are you sure?" The woman is surprised.

"Yes. It looks good on you."

"Well thank you! My name is Claudia Rivens." She takes a card from her handbag. "Here is my business card. If you have clothes you want to sell, please contact me."

She smiles and walks away.

"Stop!" shouts Kirsten. "What was the name of the website where you bought the jacket?"

Claudia stops. "I think it was called 'IFFFY'," she says. "It has three Fs. It means *I Find Fashion For You.*"

CHAPTER FOUR

When she is back in her hometown, Minty starts investigating. She looks online. She finds IFFFY. She looks at the clothes they are selling.

They are all expensive. She looks everywhere on the site. She sees one of her dresses. *The store wants $500!* she thinks. She can't believe it. She can't see any of her other clothes for sale.

There is a contact link at the bottom of the page. She sends an email to IFFFY.

---- I looked at your website. One of the dresses you are selling is mine. It was stolen from my apartment. Can you please tell me where you got it? Do you have more of my clothes? ---

Minty waits for an answer.

Dina comes back from her course the same day. Minty tells her everything that has happened. She shows Dina the website for IFFFY. She tells Dina about the message she sent to the company.

Dina is worried. "Maybe that was a bad idea," she says.

"If IFFFY broke into this apartment and stole your clothes, they are bad people. They might be dangerous. Maybe you should tell the police."

"I am telling the police," laughs Minty. "I'm telling you!"

Dina shakes her head. "I'm a junior policewoman. You must call the police station and talk to a senior person."

"Let's wait," says Minty. "Maybe they will answer my email."

Minty watches the IFFFY website. Her dress disappears. *I guess someone bought it,* thinks Minty. *They paid $500!*

Then she sees another one of her dresses for sale.

Soon after that she gets an email from IFFFY.

--- *My name is Petra Mullins. IFFFY is my company. I don't understand what you are saying! I never sell anything that is stolen! Don't say such things about my company. I want to meet you. Where do you live? I will come to see you.*---

When Dina comes home from work, Minty shows her the email.

"You mustn't tell this woman where you live! She's a bad person! She's selling stolen clothes!" says Dina.

Minty is not sure. "I don't want to go to the police until I hear her story. Maybe I can meet her in a café?"

"OK," says Dina. "But not in this town. Tell her you will meet her in Shelton. I'll come with you. You can't go alone."

Minty makes a plan to meet Petra in Shelton on Saturday afternoon. Dina is working in the morning. She comes home late. She has no time to change out of her police uniform.

They take the bus to Shelton and walk to the café. "We are a little early," says Dina. "The meeting is at three pm. It's two forty-five pm now."

They order coffees and wait. At 3:30pm, Dina says, "She's not coming. Let's go."

"No," says Minty. "Let's wait a little while."

"OK," says Dina, "But I'm bored. I'm going to look at the sea."

Twenty minutes later, a young woman hurries into the café. She looks around. She sees Minty and comes to the table. Minty is wearing her monkey and parrot coat. "You must be Minty," she says. "Your coat is so unique and so smart. I'm Petra."

She sits down. "Sorry I'm late. I live far from here. I left at six am to drive here."

"Would you like a coffee?" asks Minty. She is a little surprised. Petra is small. She has blonde hair and a sweet smile. *She doesn't look like a bad person,* thinks Minty.

Minty brings two coffees to the table. Just then, Dina walks in. She comes to the table. Petra's face goes red. Her eyes fill with tears.

"You called the police! But I haven't done anything wrong!"

Dina says, "If you haven't done anything wrong, you won't be frightened of the police! Tell us why you are selling Minty's clothes. Someone took her clothes from our apartment. Was it you?"

"No, no. I will explain. I love fashion. I find good used clothes in places like second-hand shops. I clean them and repair them. Then I sell them online," says Petra.

"Did you find Minty's clothes in a second-hand shop?" asks Dina.

"No. It was different. I saw an advertisement in the newspaper. It said ---*Excellent fashion clothes for sale. Perfect condition*---

"There was a phone number. I called and a woman said she had many clothes for sale. She sent me some pictures. They were amazing. So I called again. I said, 'I want to see them.' I met her at a train station. When I met the woman, she had two big suitcases. She sold me the clothes for five hundred dollars! She wanted cash. So I had to go to a cash machine in the station, but that was OK."

"But Petra! Didn't you think it was strange?' asked Minty.

"Well, she said her sister had died. The clothes were her sister's. We had to meet at the train station because she was going back to her hometown. I thought it was strange, but the clothes were so good! I wanted to believe her."

"I have a question," says Minty. "You have all my clothes, but you only put up one or two items on your website at a time. Why do you do that?"

Petra smiles. "Your clothes are so good! I save them. Customers see them and come back to the website. It's good business."

"You paid five hundred dollars for all the clothes, but you are selling them for much, much more than that," says Dina.

"That's good business too," says Petra. "I have made a lot of money!"

Then she says, "I can't give back the clothes I have sold, but I guess you want the rest of your clothes back, and I must give you all the money I made."

"Of course!" says Dina. "You were very silly. You will be in big trouble with the police!"

Minty is thinking. "I have an idea," she says. "I met a woman who was wearing a jacket she bought from you. She looked great! She likes it. She said, 'other people like it too'. That made me happy.

"I have new ideas for clothes now. I'm making different things. Maybe you can keep my clothes and sell them online. But you must say 'Made by Minty'."

Petra looks very happy. "That would be great! I can do that."

"And you must pay Minty every time you sell something she made," says Dina.

"Oh, yes!" says Petra. "I will give Minty twenty-five percent. That's a lot of money."

"No!" shouts Dina. "You have to pay Minty fifty percent! We will watch your website. We will know!"

"OK," says Petra. "I will give Minty fifty percent."

Minty and Petra exchange information.

Then Dina and Minty leave the café to walk to the bus station. They walk past Alice's Home Designs. Alice is looking out the shop window. She sees Minty. *That's the monkey and parrot curtain material. The young woman made it into a coat! It looks very good. I will ask her about her friend,* she thinks.

Alice runs into the street. "Hello!" she shouts to Minty.

"Oh, Alice. Nice to see you again. Are you OK?" says Minty.

"You and your friend helped me so much. And I didn't ask your names."

"I'm Minty. This is my friend Dina," says Minty.

"But your other friend? She is so clever. I want to ask her to come and work for me. How can I contact her?"

Minty knows that it is not a good idea to give information like telephone numbers and addresses. "Her name is Kirsten. I'll tell her to call you."

"OK. Thank you," says Alice.

CHAPTER FIVE

Dina and Minty take the bus back home. They walk to their apartment. Minty is pleased and excited. "We solved the mystery!" she says. "And now I will get a lot of money from IFFFY."

Dina is not happy. "Petra is silly. She likes money too much. But I don't think she is a bad person. But who was the woman at the train station? I'm a policewoman. I will tell the story to my boss at the police station."

Dina talks to her boss. Her boss says, "Petra Mullins broke the law. You cannot buy stolen things. But I agree with you. She is not a bad person. She wanted to believe the story about the dead sister because she is interested in money. I want to catch the woman from the train station."

He smiles at Dina. "You are junior, but I think you will be a very good policewoman. This is your first case. Find the woman who sold the clothes!"

Dina calls Petra. "Tell me the day and time you met the woman at the railway station. Tell me the place you met her."

Petra says, "It was November thirteenth. We met at eleven am. We met near the bookstore. There are some seats outside the store."

"Thank you," says Dina.

There are security cameras everywhere in the railway station, thinks Dina.

She finds the security camera records for the railway station on that day and time. She watches the video. *Oh no!* she thinks. *I can see Petra very well, but the woman with the suitcases was very clever. She was wearing a coat with a hood. I can't see her face.*

Dina watches the video again. She sees Petra go away. She sees Petra come back with the money. Then she sees something interesting. The woman puts out her hand to take the money. There is a tattoo on her hand. It is a black snake.

Maybe that tattoo is important. Maybe someone will know what it means, she thinks.

Dina talks to an expert in the police station. "I know this tattoo," he says. "There is a gang that has this tattoo. So I think the woman must be a member of that gang."

"Where do they live?" asks Dina. "What are their names?"

The expert laughs. "It's not easy. We don't know. The name of the gang is Death Snake. One member of the gang is in prison, but he won't tell you anything."

Dina reads all the police reports. The police think the Death Snake gang has four members. They break into houses and apartments. They steal televisions and computers. They sell them online or in pubs and bars. They use different names. They all have the snake tattoo, but there is no more information. Dina doesn't know what to do.

Minty joins Petra's company. Every week Petra sends Minty half the money from the sales. Minty is very happy but she is also surprised.

"Petra sent me photographs of all my stolen clothes, so that we can set the price. But some of my clothes are not there," she says to Dina. "Three skirts and a jacket are missing."

"Maybe the woman from the gang sold them to other people," says Dina. "Or maybe she kept the skirts and jacket for herself."

One Friday evening, Kirsten calls Dina. "I tried to call Minty, but she didn't answer her phone."

"No," says Dina. "Minty went to her parents' house for the weekend. Her grandmother is sick in hospital. If Minty is in the hospital, maybe she has turned her phone off."

Kirsten is excited. "I saw a woman on the street. She was wearing one of Minty's skirts! She caught a bus. I'm following the bus on my bike."

"Kirsten! Be careful!" Dina is worried. "It might be dangerous."

"When she gets off the bus, I will talk to her. It's OK."

"No! Maybe she is a member of the gang who broke into our apartment," says Dina. "Where are you? What is the number of the bus?"

"I'm in a traffic jam on the corner of Main Street and Crown Road. I'm behind the bus. The bus is number four three seven."

"OK," says Dina. "I'll come and find you. Don't go near the woman! And don't use your phone when you are riding your bike!"

Dina has a motorbike. She rides into town.

CHAPTER SIX

The traffic jam on Main Street has gone, but there is a lot of traffic, and it is moving very slowly. Dina can't see Kirsten.

The bus stops at the city bus station. Dina parks her motorbike and runs to the bus. There are many women getting off the bus.

Which one is the woman? thinks Dina. Then she sees a woman wearing a skirt with yellow sunflowers and green beads. *That's her!* she thinks. *That's the woman Kirsten saw. Does she have the snake tattoo? She is too far away. I can't see.*

The woman is meeting two men. They stand and talk. Dina calls her boss. "I'm at the city bus station. Maybe some members of the Death Snake gang are here."

"OK," says her boss. "You are alone, so don't go near them. Watch them. I'll send a police car."

"OK, boss. I'll wait for them."

Then Dina sees Kirsten. She is running towards the two men and the woman. "Hi!" shouts Kirsten. "Why are you wearing my friend's skirt? Did you take it from her apartment?"

The woman laughs. "Yes, I liked it! So I kept it."

"Why did you tell her!" one of the men shouts at the woman. "Now we will have to stop her from talking!" He takes Kirsten's arm and pulls her towards the road.

Oh no! Maybe he will push her under a bus! I have to do something, thinks Dina.

Dina runs towards them. Kirsten is screaming. All the people in the bus station are looking, but no one does anything.

"Police," shouts Dina. The other man hits Dina in the face, but Dina kicks him in the stomach. He falls back onto the ground. Dina jumps on him. Then the woman jumps on top of Dina. She is very heavy, so Dina can't breathe.

Kirsten is still screaming and kicking. The other man tries to punch her, but she hits his face very hard. He falls over.

Suddenly there is the sound of police sirens. There is shouting. Someone pulls the woman off Dina's back. She stands up. Two policemen are holding the woman. She is shouting many bad words. Dina can see her hand. It has the black snake tattoo. Two more policemen take hold of the man on the ground. He also has the tattoo.

Dina and Kirsten go to the police station. Dina's boss is there. He is angry with Dina. "I told you to watch!" he says. "Why did you attack those gang members?"

"I'm sorry," says Kirsten. "It was my fault. I was so excited. I shouted at them. Then one of the men attacked me! Dina was very brave. She came to help me."

"OK," says Dina's boss. "I understand."

He smiles at the two young women. "We caught three gang members today. That's good!"

On Sunday night, Minty comes back to the apartment. "How is your grandmother?" asks Dina.

"She is much better. She will leave the hospital soon," says Minty.

The doorbell rings. "We have a visitor," says Minty. "I wonder who it is?"

She opens the door. It is Kirsten. "I asked Kirsten to come tonight," says Dina. "We have many things to tell you."

Dina and Kirsten tell Minty everything that happened on Friday.

"It's great!" says Kirsten. "I'm sorry you lost your clothes, but it was good luck. I have a part-time job at Alice's shop. When I graduate, she will give me a full-time job."

"Petra is selling my clothes online and I have money in the bank!" laughs Minty.

"And my boss is very pleased because we caught the Black Snake gang. Thank you, Kirsten!" says Dina. "And…"

"And?" Minty doesn't know what Dina means.

"Remember the woman we met at the fashion show? The woman who bought your jacket?" asks Kirsten. "She gave you her business card."

"Yes, I remember," says Minty.

"Dina found her business card on your desk. She called the woman to tell her the story," says Kirsten.

"She was very interested. She was also very pleased." Dina is smiling. "She entered your jacket in an international fashion design competition, and it won! She didn't know your name or contact details, so she couldn't tell you. But the competition prize was five thousand dollars. Losing your clothes was the best thing that ever happened!"

THANK YOU

Thank you for reading Made by Minty. We hope you enjoyed the story. (Word count: 4,697)

If you would like to read more graded readers, please visit our website http://www.italkyoutalk.com

Other Level 2 graded readers include
Adventure in Rome
Andre's Dream
A New Life
A Passion for Music
Christmas Tales
Danger in Seattle
Don't Come Back
Dressed for Success
Elspeth and the Visitor
Finders Keepers…
How Did You Meet?
Hunted in Hong Kong
John Sees a Murder
Marcy's Bakery
Men's Konkatsu Tales
Message in a Bottle
Murder on Whale Island

Neighbours
Salaryman Secrets!
Stories for Halloween
The Cruise Ship
The Perfect Wedding
The House in the Forest
The Kindness of Strangers
The School on Bolt Street
The Secret Door
Tiffany and Max Investigate
Train Travel
Trouble in Paris
Who's There?
Women's Konkatsu Tales

ABOUT THE AUTHOR

I Talk You Talk Press is an award-winning Japan-based publisher of language textbooks, graded readers and language learning/teaching resources. We won the Language Learner Literature Award in 2019 and 2020.

Our team is made up of highly experienced language teachers and translators, who have all studied at least one additional language to an advanced level.

This experience enables us to design our materials from the perspective of both the teacher and the learner. We consult with both teachers and language learners when designing our textbooks and graded readers, and test our materials extensively in the classroom before publication.

We are a fast-growing press, and currently publish graded readers for learners of English. We publish new graded readers monthly.

www.ingramcontent.com/pod-product-compliance
Lightning Source LLC
La Vergne TN
LVHW042241190726
843491LV00003BA/1177

* 9 7 8 4 9 1 0 9 7 1 1 7 9 *